I0414921

This Book Belongs To:

BY
Home Planners And Journals

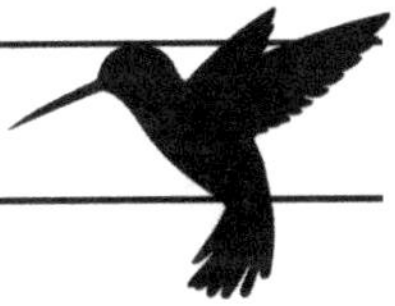

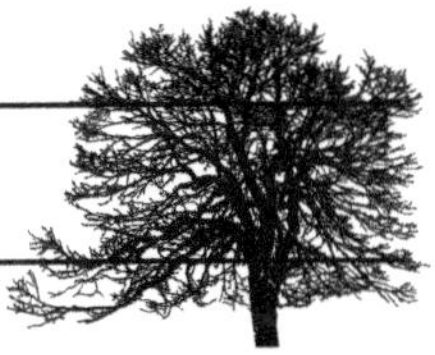

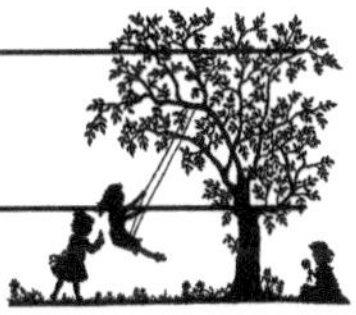

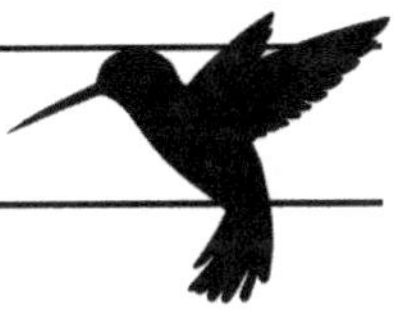

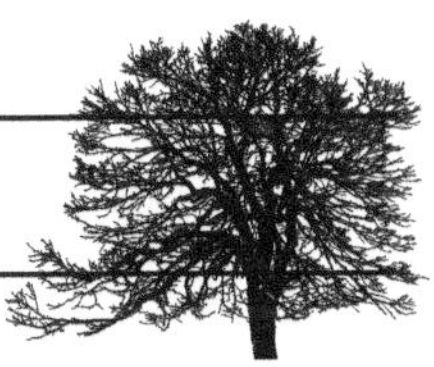

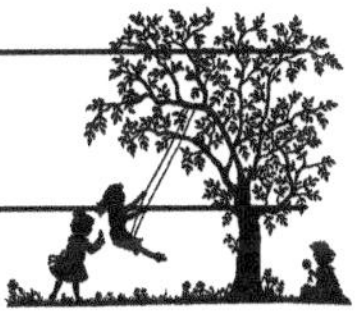

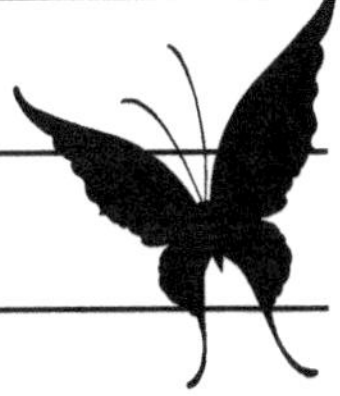

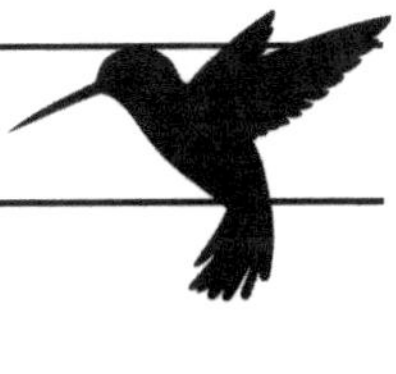

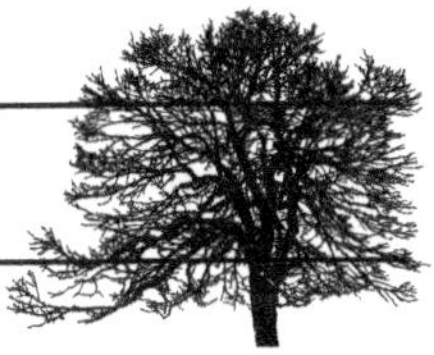

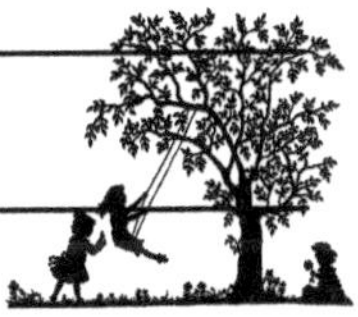

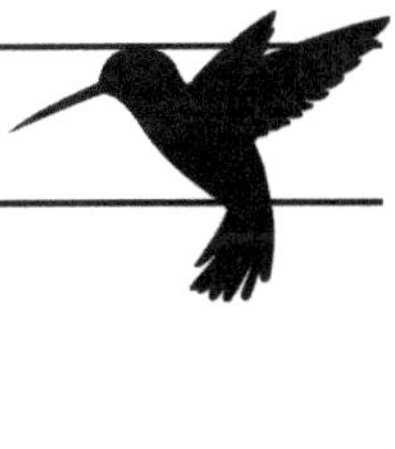

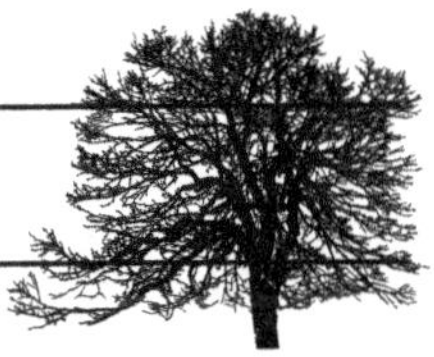

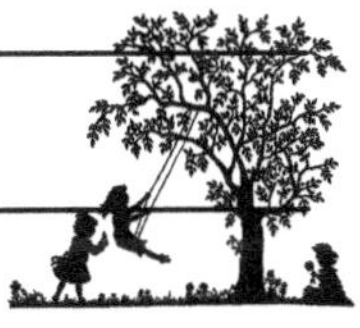

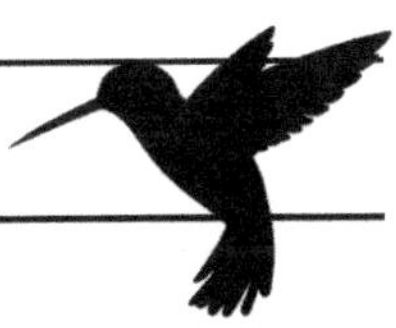

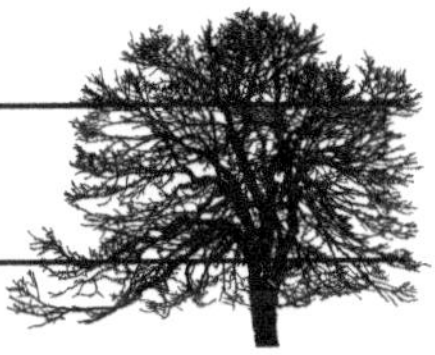

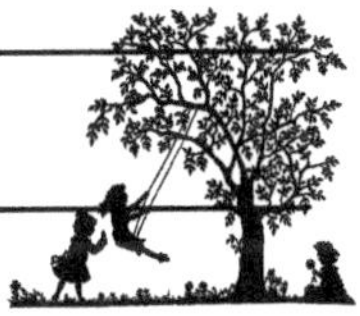

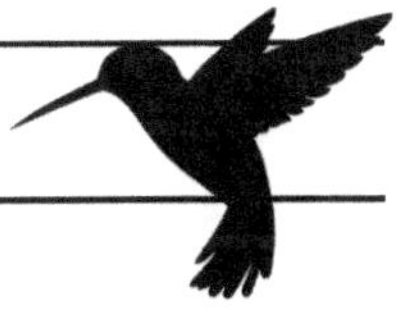

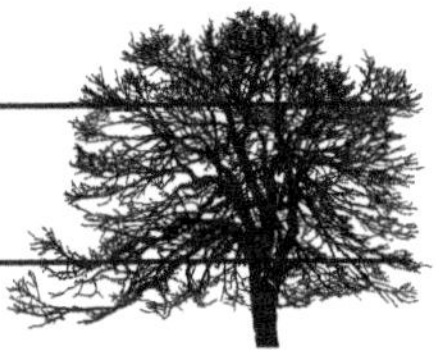

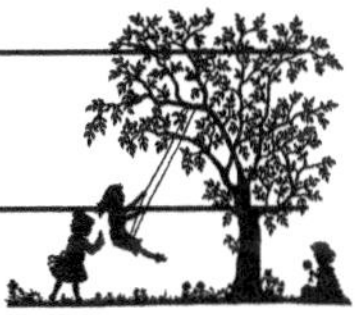

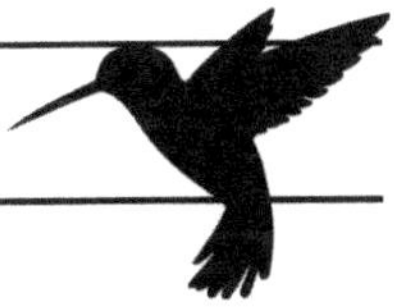

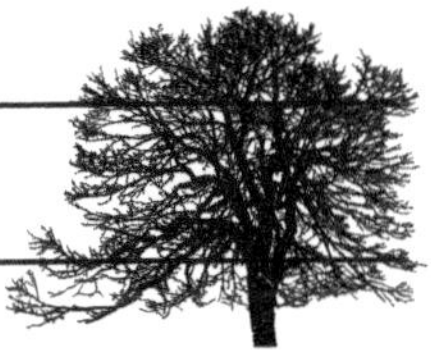

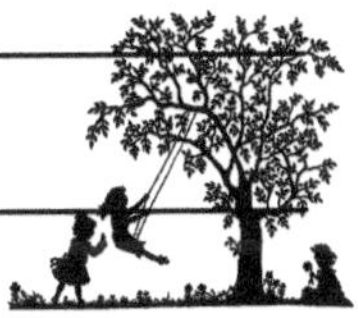

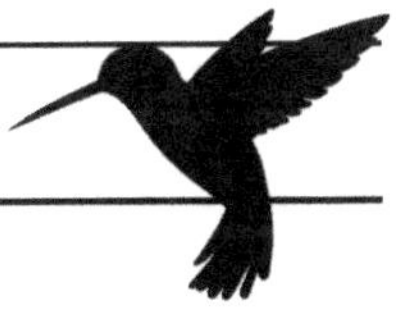

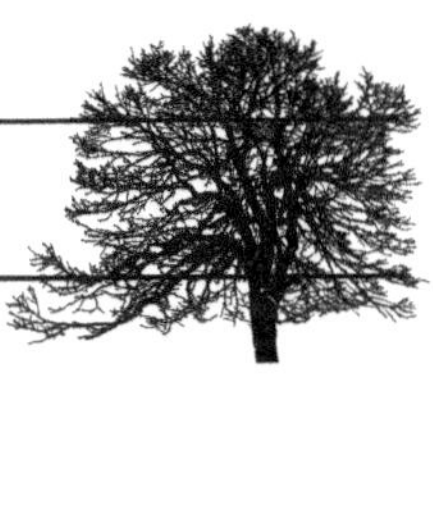

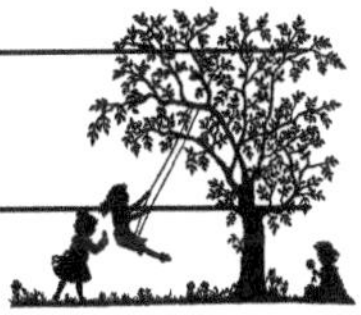

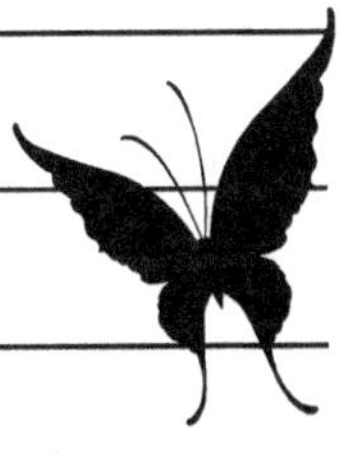

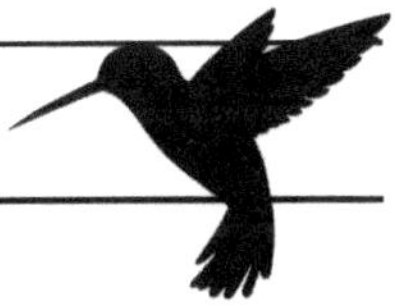

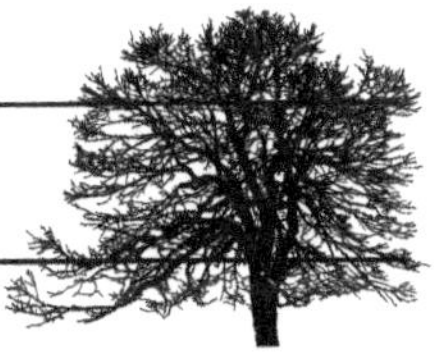

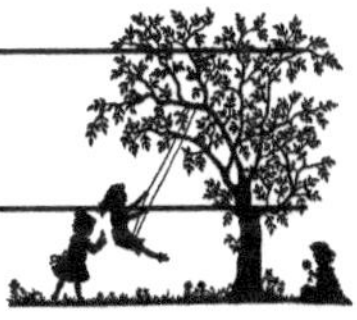

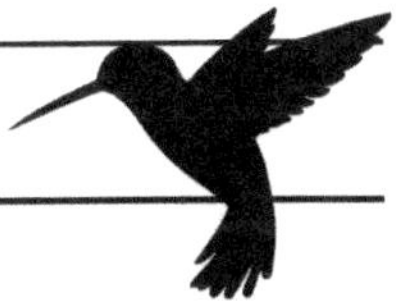

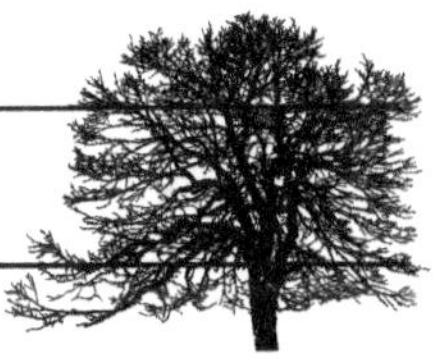

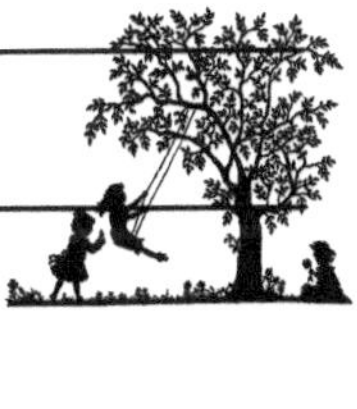

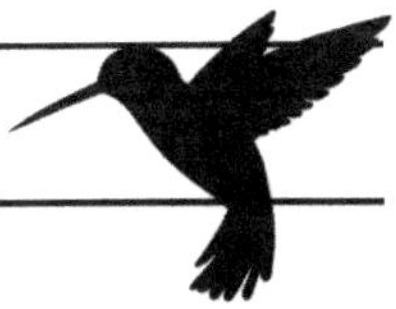

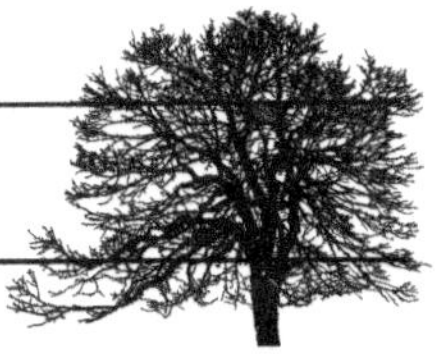

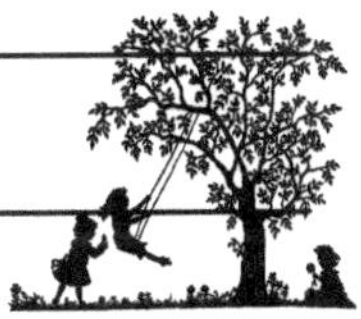

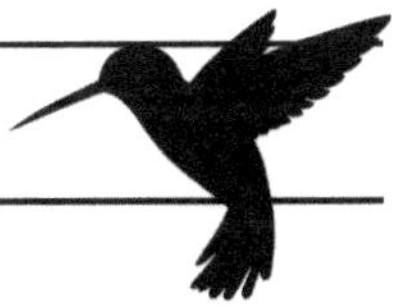

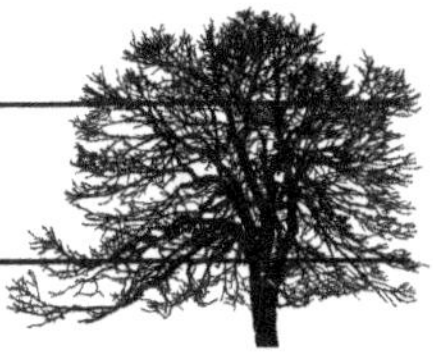

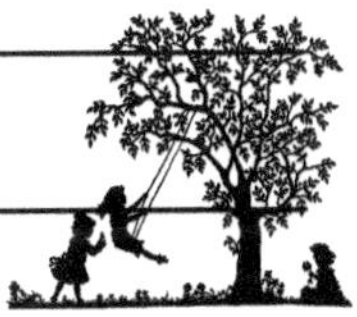

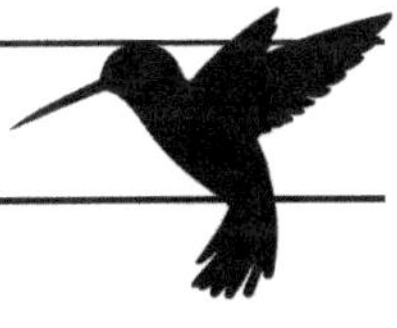

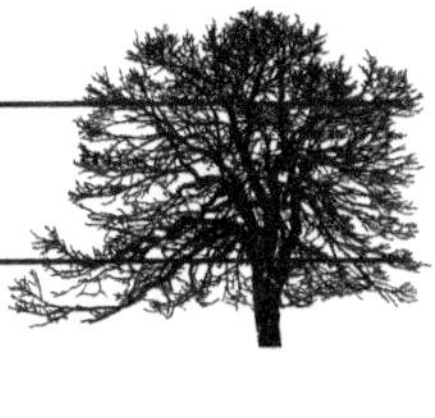

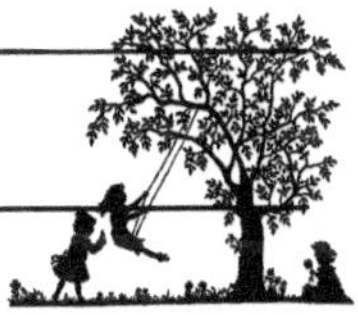

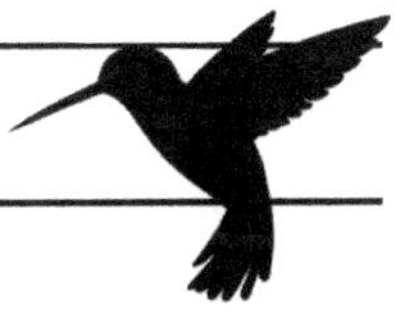

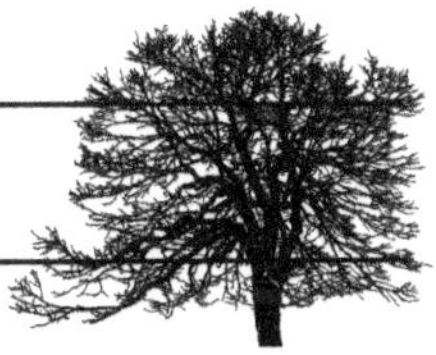

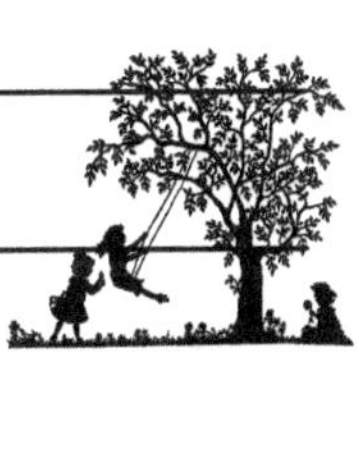

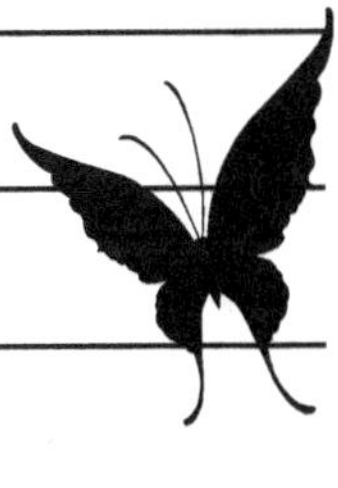

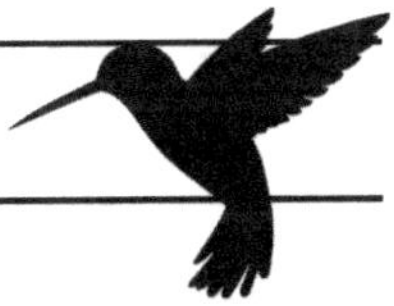

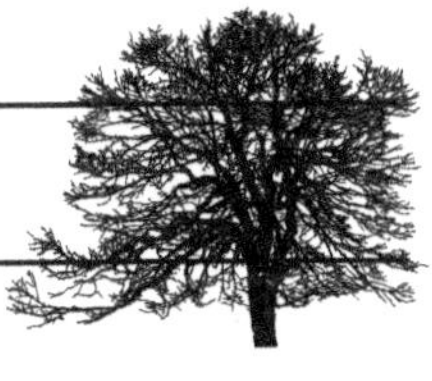

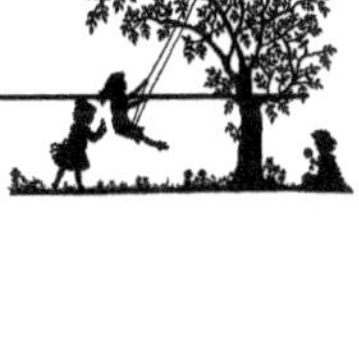

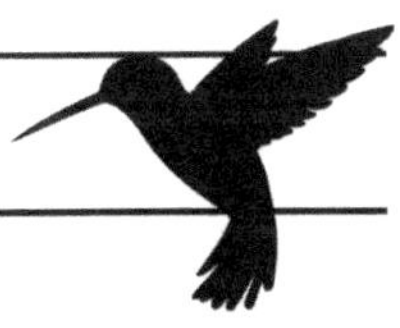

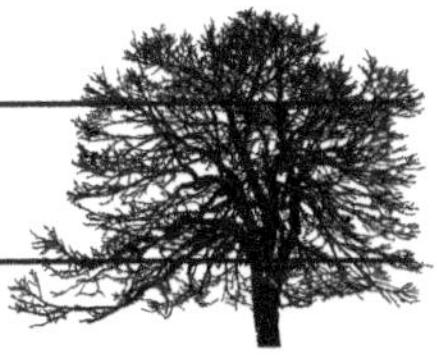

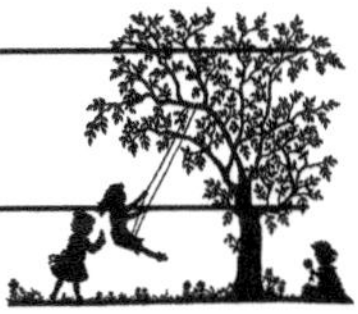

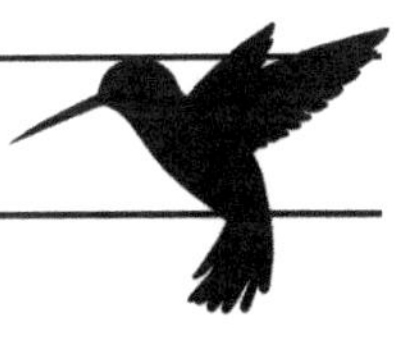

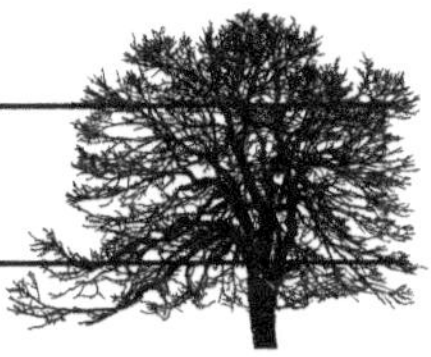

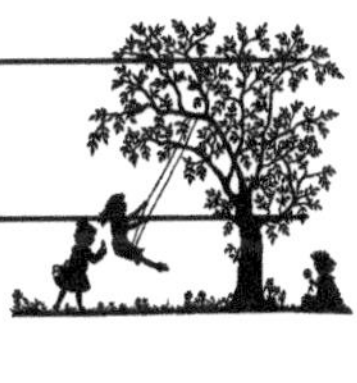

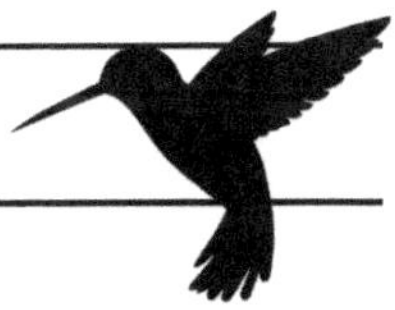

www.ingramcontent.com/pod-product-compliance
Lightning Source LLC
Chambersburg PA
CBHW072051280526
45788CB00006B/2259
9781090231277